Endorsements

"Baker has developed a deeply held passion for personally knowing God. He is zealous to have you experience the goodness, kindness, and greatness of our everlasting Lord. Dig in and delight yourself In the abundance that truly knowing God can bring to your life."

Jeff Graf,
Founder, Mission Connections

"If you find yourself wondering why life has not given you the satisfaction you were hoping for, then this book is a must. Even if you simply find yourself longing for more meaning as you Look at your life, this book is for you."

Bob Allums,
Director, A Praying Life Ministries

"It's no surprise that Baker Taylor's work "Is That All That There IS?" deeply encourages and wisely counsels. It reflects the journey and counsel Baker lives and shares on his pilgrimage with the Lord. For solid, practical insight and wisdom for daily living, Baker has given us a helpful guide. Hope you enjoy it as I have!"

Christopher Faith,
Pastor/Elder, Blacksburg Christian Fellowship

IS THAT
ALL
THERE IS?

IS THAT ALL THERE IS?

Do you worry?
Do you feel lonely?
Does God answer you?

Do you really know the life-giving, loving, caring, sacrificing God who created you?

Read this book, and it and the Holy Spirit will encourage you to know Him for yourself.

BAKER TAYLOR

XULON PRESS

Xulon Press
2301 Lucien Way #415
Maitland, FL 32751
407.339.4217
www.xulonpress.com

© 2022 by Baker Taylor

All rights reserved solely by the author. The author guarantees all contents are original and do not infringe upon the legal rights of any other person or work. No part of this book may be reproduced in any form without the permission of the author.

Due to the changing nature of the Internet, if there are any web addresses, links, or URLs included in this manuscript, these may have been altered and may no longer be accessible. The views and opinions shared in this book belong solely to the author and do not necessarily reflect those of the publisher. The publisher therefore disclaims responsibility for the views or opinions expressed within the work.

Unless otherwise indicated, Scripture quotations taken from the New King James Version (NKJV). Copyright © 1982 by Thomas Nelson, Inc. Used by permission. All rights reserved.

Paperback ISBN-13: 978-1-6628-4096-8
Ebook ISBN-13: 978-1-6628-4097-5

Thank You

I need to give thanks to the people who assisted me in writing my first book. Jeff Graf, Bob Allums, Sandy Young and Chris Faith each reviewed my manuscript with many helpful suggestions, and gave me much encouragement while I was writing. Also Jeff Highfield, who graciously answered his phone each time I called asking questions regarding something from the Bible or where to find it. Then there is my wife, Pauline, who consistently answered any question I asked her, gave suggestions, and helped me overcome my difficulties on the computer. I also don't want to overlook all those who prayed for me. I received blessing after blessing while writing, " Is That All There Is."

J. Baker Taylor

IS THAT ALL THERE IS?

Back in 1969, there was a song by Peggy Lee named, "Is That All There Is." A lot of us may not be able to remember that far back, but the song reminisced about many things in life that don't come out as expected. That can be said by anyone, regardless of who they are or what stage of life they are in. How about a student about to finish their studies, or a businessperson considering where he or she may be at that time in their career, or a parent thinking, "Will I ever get through all this?" Even a Christian believer wondering, "Is that all there is to my Christian life?"

There can come a time when any one of us could say to him or herself: "Am I really where I should be?" "Who really am I?" "Am I functioning how I know I should?" These are important questions that I couldn't or shouldn't try to answer for anyone else, but you may want to ask yourself. However, I would like to address this from a Christian's perspective as we go along.

The spiritual side of who we are is the most vital part for us to consider. It contributes to how we think, our reactions, what our priorities are, our values, the way we talk, how we spend our money, how we use our time, and "Where is my life headed?" Many people have decided that becoming a Christian can and will be the best and most fulfilling way to live now and to know their eternal destination. This is what God intended.

This decision brings about changes and patterns in lives that can be full of joy, hope, and satisfaction. This is the beginning of a new life or chapter of our lives. As life goes on, we can become aware of some shortcomings or patterns of life that haven't been modified or changed as we thought they would have. I am sorry to say, some of these patterns are not being considered or are unaddressed. These concerns can and will set patterns that will rob you of becoming the person God created you to be.

Many of us become part of a fellowship of like believers, where we can hear more about God and the Christian life. These could include adult education, various ministries, youth activities, choir participation, and other activities that ought to become satisfying experiences. This could lead us into becoming joyful and fulfilled everyday Christians. As we grow, we may become teachers, deacons, elders and other leaders in the church. This is normal and helps Christians grow.

What may be missing? How about a vital, satisfying relationship with God the Father, Jesus Christ His Son, and the Holy Spirit? We must have this to be the Christian that God created us to be. The scripture confirms this belief. Sometimes we, who really love God, forget that the Holy Spirit is in us on a day-to-day basis. He loves us, and He is continually wanting to comfort us and guide us. If only we would see Him as who He really is.

Our God is the Creator, the one who made us "*in His own image*" (Gen. 1:27). Think of that! What does that mean to you? Have you given that very much thought? He created the world, the stars, the heavens, and all that is in it. That includes you and I, His children! (See Psalm 139:15-17.)

He has a plan for each of us as believers in Jesus Christ, our Lord and Savior. He desires that we live a godly life and equips us, when Jesus enters into our lives, through the presence of the Holy Spirit. This Holy Spirit leads us into a lifetime of reading, studying, and sharing to learn more about the Triune God, the Three in One (God the Father, God the Son, and God the Holy Spirit). In the process, we learn to trust and to obey God more and more.

There are many ways He does that, but primarily through our following His principles. That is a sure way to become "all" that God wants you to be. Meaning, as we pursue this journey, our love for Him continues to grow even beyond our imagination.

I just read Jeremiah 29:11. *"For I know the thoughts that I think toward you, says the Lord, thoughts of peace and not of evil, to give you a future and a hope."* Wow! What an incredible God. And one more statement of God's plan for believers. He said, *"And if I go and prepare a place for you, I will come again and receive you to Myself; that where I am, that you may be also"* (John 14:3).

For a while I have been thinking that there seems to be **something missing** in the Christian community. We all know that we live in a time of much news and confusion. There are thoughts and discussion about health care, economics, local and world news and safety. We also live with normal day-to-day concerns and activities. We may be working, in school, shopping, dining, going to church, finding entertainment, and enjoying the good life. Sometimes I wonder: "Where is God in all of this? Where is our joy? How well do I know Him? How personal is my relationship with Him? How do I depend on Him? How much do I trust Him? Do I really trust Him?" You may notice that I went from "we" to "I" with my questions.

You see, I had to ask myself these questions. Well, I know unquestionably that God loves me! He has shown me His love through His Word and my daily walk with Him. That's the way it should be. We know He loves us, but does He know that we love Him? If we believe in God, we surely know God understands how much we love Him. That could bring us to think, "How much do I love God?"

I'm not trying to put tit for tat or good works into the picture, but look at the marital relationship that many of us have. We usually know our spouses love us. Do our spouses know we love them? Maybe we haven't paid enough attention to them, and they wonder. Do they know how much we really love them? So too, I know God loves me even beyond my imagination. Am I showing Him how much I love Him? I think it's time to reflect and pray about how I am showing God how I love Him. You know what? That's not the right question. The right question is, "Do I love God as I should?"

I believe we first see God as someone who can fulfill our present needs. It could be through our loneliness, disappointments, fears, needing love or providing material wants or needs. We may begin to see Him as the God who knows and sees all and wants to guide us through all. Hopefully, we learn that He loves us unconditionally, He is committed to caring for us and has prepared a place for our eternity while He transforms us in this earthly life.

How much time am I giving God? Well, I pray regularly, I read the Bible often, and I think about Him when I can. Then one day, I read what God said in His Word, *"Let us make man in our image, according to Our likeness; let them have dominion over the fish of the sea, over the birds of the air, and over the cattle, over all the earth and over every creeping thing that creeps on the earth." So, God created man in His own image;*

in the image of God, He created him; male and female He created them"' (Gen. 1:26-27).

Maybe I should start thinking about who God is and what that means to me. When He created me in His own image, He must have had a very special plan for me, thinks highly of me, and knows how He will equip me so that His ideal for me can be fulfilled. He has given us dominion over the earth and knows that I would be a rightful heir of God as long as I know and accept Jesus Christ as my Savior. He has foreknown and predestined us, and as believers, we are now brethren in Christ. What else could a person want? In John 14:1-2, Jesus tells us *"Let not your heart be troubled; you believe in God, believe also in me. In My Father's house are many mansions; if it were not so, I would have told you. I go to prepare a place for you."* What a promise. As we read God's Word and accept Jesus Christ as our savior, we are not only saved, but we are believers. Praise Him in all things, and thank Him for the incredible promises He has given us.

There are natural expectations when we become part of any organization or team. This is also true in becoming a Christian and joining the body of Christ. You need commitment, education, growth, and determination in order to fulfill the reason you are there and to be part of its purpose.

Promises/Faithfulness

The more I read God's Word, there is much confirmation of Him being incredibly faithful and what I would call a "promise keeper." The Lord is faithful to all His promises and loving. Here are just a few of those scriptures:

- *"Blessed be the Lord, who has given rest to His people Israel, according to all that He promised. There has*

> not failed one word of all His good promise, which He promised through His servant Moses" (1 Kgs. 8:56).
> - "Therefore, know that the Lord your God, He is God, the faithful God who keeps covenant and mercy for a thousand generations with those who love Him and keep His commandments" (Deut. 7:9).
> - "God who is faithful, by whom you were called into the fellowship of His Son, Jesus Christ our Lord" (2 Cor. 1:9).
> - "But the Lord is faithful, who will establish you and guard you from the evil one" (2 Thess. 3:3).
> - "Beloved, do not think it strange concerning the fiery trial which is to try you, as though some strange thing happened to you, but rejoice to the extent that you partake of Christ's sufferings, that when His glory is revealed, you may be glad with exceeding joy." (1 Pet. 4: 12-13)

When we see the reality of His faithfulness and promises in our daily lives, we should then thank and praise Him for the truth of His Word. That builds our understanding of Him and heightens our joy in being a Christian. As we recap our day during our evening prayer, it is good we thank Him for the number of times we have sensed Him throughout our day. If you are not sensing Him, you need to talk with Him about this. This reinforces our awareness of God's presence in our lives and deepens our love for Him.

Faith

Let's take a look at the word "faith." It could mean having confidence, believing, or trust. We all have faith in something or someone. Why do we have this faith in anything? As I look at life, we just can't get through without faith. It is the essence of hope, and we don't have much chance for happiness, peace, or satisfaction without hope. We hope our car starts when we turn the key. We hope the store has what we need. We hope for things every day. We hope the doctor or dentist is proficient in what they are helping us with. Then we trust the bridge will hold us and the cars. It would be great if all this could be based on belief.

But I have found the only thing in life that is steadfast and consistent is God, who is thoroughly described in His Word, the Bible. It has held up for thousands of years under incredible and reliable amounts of examination and criticism by mostly learned people.

In gaining hope, trust, and belief, our consideration must be based on truth. Seeking and believing God turns into faith. The Bible says in Hebrews 11:1, *"Now faith is the substance of things hoped for, the evidence of things not seen."* With this faith, we believe in God and trust in all His attributes, promises, and declarations. By this we also find joy, hope, and peace which changes our perspective in life. This is what God wants to see in us. But don't overlook trust and obedience which is some of the evidence that we truly love Him.

Fear

Throughout God's Word, He is telling us to fear not. Our God is always truthful and a realist. He understands the various pains and fears we may have but has told us in Isaiah 41:10, *"Fear not, for I am with you; Be not dismayed, for I am your God. I will strengthen you, Yes, I will help you, I will uphold you with my righteous right hand."* We cannot change things that have already happened, but He can and will comfort us if we will let Him and trust Him to bring peace to difficult situations.

Too often we try to do things ourselves while not being aware of what God may be doing. This can be for ourselves or others. We can also pray for God to intercede and alter situations to avoid pain or other concerns, but remember, He has His ways and purposes to draw us closer to Him. God certainly knows we have a tendency to fear or He wouldn't include this word or similar thoughts hundreds of times in the Bible. Remember, God is the Master in grace and comfort of which we need continually.

Forgiveness

Another major fact is God has forgiven all our sins. *"In Him we have redemption through His blood, the forgiveness of sins, according to the riches of His grace which He made to abound toward us in all wisdom and prudence"* (Eph. 1:7-8). This is a promise that has given me incredible faith. God not only has forgiven us for all our shortcomings, He also wants to see us forgive others as we have been forgiven. We know this can be very difficult, but we look at ourselves and consider our tendencies to sin and neglect and how God is continuing to forgive us. We should be happy to forgive others. This kind of thinking sets us free. Thank God for His incredible plan to set us free.

Our Battle, the Sin Nature

We have a sin nature and will have it until we die. As Christians, most likely, we will not engage in sins such as rage, murder, rape, and other such serious sins, but we still may be prone to cheating, lying, gossiping, deceiving, and the like. We are assured of His forgiveness by accepting Jesus Christ as our Savior (John 3:16). But with God's help, we can fight these things, according to His Word, as we perceive how much God loves us and praise Him for His love and forgiveness.

This comes from intimately KNOWING Him. Many of us read God's Word on a pretty regular basis which should help us grow in understanding Him. We can live through the pitfalls of life and feel like this is the way it is, all while accepting our bumps and bruises. Or, we can see God's love and mercy for us as we intimately live with Him, while not letting the many distractions or sufferings in life take our hearts and focus off Him. You must know and trust God is rejoicing at your growth in overcoming this sin nature. You need to rejoice with God!

Self vs God

We all have needs and desires. They come from our different backgrounds and experiences that others may not understand. They can get us into trouble, either with other people or with ourselves. We learn to work our way around some of these differences and other times they become difficult, stress-ladened problems. We have grown to want things "our way or the highway." That saying sounds cute, however, it can be very destructive. If we let it, this kind of thinking can and will crowd into our spirit. Now think about what this says: *"I thank God through Jesus Christ our Lord! So then, with the mind I myself serve the law of God, but with the flesh the law of sin"* (Rom. 7:25). This is very important. It says we have a choice, God or flesh! We have a sin nature that can be overcome by the power of the Spirit of God, who comes to abide in us when we accepted Jesus Christ as our Lord and Savior.

We all have a self that looks out for self. Without bringing God into our lives in a personal and intimate way, self will take over and our sin nature will replace God's role of directing and guiding. This can be tough to deal with, but it is true. Our sin nature wants to please us with whatever it takes, oftentimes without considering what effect that has on us or others. This type of "please me" thinking will often become very repugnant.

Often, we rationalize these actions which deadens our conscience. The more it rules, the less voice and influence God will have in our lives. But God has shown us the answer. The more we see and receive the love God has for us and trust Him, the less self will need and want to control us. This builds into incredible peace. With this comes confidence, godly self-control, and joy. It is tough to say but we must, through God's help, defeat self's strangling grip on us.

After accepting Jesus Christ, we have the power to overcome these sin tendencies, however, the decisions to use this God-given power is up to us. The more we believe and trust God, we will use these incredible tools He has given us. Galatians 5:24 says, *"And those who are Christ's have crucified the flesh with its passions and desires."* Now go on to verse 25: *"If we live in the Sprit, let us also walk in the Spirit."* God, overall, is leading us to stand strong and walk in our belief in Him, to be all that He wants us to be, being guided by the Spirit.

Small Group Participation

Small group participation is also a great way to grow. Some include only married couples and many are exclusive to male or female. Some may focus on unmarried couples or certain age groups. Don't let this stop you from praying to God for His leading in finding a group. This can bring together people with similar life concerns. Many are currently functioning or could be established by just a few interested people. If established correctly, it will be a place where we can learn to become vulnerable in sharing and trusting in each other.

"What is said here, stays here" is often an unstated assumption. I am part of a group of men who exemplified this thinking. We share feelings, ideas, and positions that may differ, all while discussing our lives and God in our lives. Yet, we love and respect each other more as we continue our regular meetings. You will praise God as you see a brother or sister unburdened and set free from things that can hold any of us back. We Christians can mature and grow in these environments.

Devotionals

Reading devotional books reinforces my vision and understanding of what God is saying. A good devotional author takes God's Word and gives wonderful examples and insight to what God is saying. They can be more enlightening and inspirational than academic.

I was planning to include a few examples of devotionals but decided to share with you the impact they have on me. For the past eight years, my wife and I have been doing devotions together. We are blessed by the encouragement and insight they bring to us. So often we gain a new perspective by reading devotionals accompanied with scripture, which may or may not be familiar to us. We can feel overwhelmed by how timely and to the point they speak directly to one or both of us.

It is obvious to my wife the amount of growth and understanding I show, particularly in the Old Testament. I remember first reading the OT and having a hard time understanding what God was trying to say to me here and now. It is very eye opening and a blessing to have devotional writers help me understand God's message. This past year, we read daily from two devotional books. Dr. Charles Stanley's books are very biblically inspired and practical in application. I would also recommend Paul David Tripp, whose writings are a little more lengthy and very rich in meaning and insight.

The writings continue to deepen my understanding, faith, and love for our heavenly Father. Devotional reading brings thoughts about ourselves and God that I/we haven't thought about before. Many times, they are very timely.

Wisdom

"Happy is the man that finds wisdom, and the man that gains understanding" (Pro. 5:13). You see, wisdom is not a by-product of age or experience. As we learn to depend more and more upon God and ask for His wisdom, God directs us. He just wants our relationship to be totally dependent on Him as we love, trust, and joyfully obey our incredible God.

He shows in Proverbs 2:1-11 the potential He sees in wisdom. Proverbs 3:1-35 is another chapter where God speaks to us regarding applications of wisdom. The frankest thing I should say is that God's wisdom and the world's wisdom are very different. A lot of our general wisdom can be practical; godly wisdom is embedded in biblical truth and is the spiritual foundation.

An Experience

Besides reading God's Word, we also have opportunities to see it in action. One morning in December, while leaving my home, I noticed it had been snowing and icing a little. After taking my first step down the stairs off my porch, I went flying and landed on my back. To make a long story short, after being taken to two hospitals, I ended up in a hospital one and a half hours from home with a collapsed lung, fractured back bone, and broken ribs. Needless to say, it was a very painful experience.

That evening I had to lie on my back to sleep. The pain became very acute. I didn't want to take the pain medication nurses brought me because of my fear of potential drug side effects, and I started talking with God. I didn't feel I was praying because I knew how bad I felt and just needed to talk with Him. After a short time talking with God, I noticed the pain had subsided. I couldn't believe what was happening but I sure started thanking and praising Him. Well, after two more evenings of pain and talking with God, each time with the same results, I knew what God was saying when He said, *"I will not forsake or leave you"* (Heb. 5:6).

What I'm saying in these notes is that God showed me His incomparable love, mercy, and comfort in a very crucial time. This thinking is imbedded in my heart no matter what my circumstances may be. God promises He will be with us through all the trauma we may face. This could be illness, loss of a loved one, injury, or a great disappointment. But God will help us get through these difficult times. We give this advice to others when they go through adversities and suffering. We need to remember this advice for ourselves as well when we go through them.

I have also found I don't need to keep asking Him over and over to forgive me for my short sightedness or sins but to help me fight my weaknesses and sins. The more I believe and trust in Him, the more my life seems to get richer and the more many of my weaker characteristics are fading as God intends them to. Praise God!

I have come to believe many of us are not looking at the "fullness" of God. Maybe we just haven't spent enough quality time with Him to truly know and trust Him. Or, possibly, we are not looking for Him throughout our day. Consequently, this lack of fully knowing or understanding all of who God is or what He has in store for us could lead us into an unfulfilled Christian life, missing out on much of what God has planned for us. We don't want to miss any of God's promises. *"But seek* first the kingdom of God and His righteousness and all these things shall be added unto you" (Mat. 6:33).

Prayer

At thirty years old, I found it awkward to pray to God as a new, serious Christian. It seemed like I was trying to maintain communications with someone I couldn't see. I had made my commitment to God, but how deep was it? It took me a while to understand how God spoke to me. Most of us were told much about prayer and just how vital it was. God speaks to us through His Word, the Bible, and others we may seek counsel through.

As we begin understanding God and how He intends for us to live, I see how He can communicate with us also through prayer. While growing, I also realized God's timing regarding my various requests or petitions were not always the same as mine. God can often speak to us through times of just thinking. We can see this as our conscience speaking or just through someone else. Either way, it very well could be God speaking to us. We also become aware of the fact that God has a perfect will for us as well as perfect timing. We never want to overlook the fact that God wants the best for us.

I, in my juvenile way of thinking, have found that I am very comfortable "talking" with my heavenly Father. He has promised to show us the way, but not necessarily whether I should buy a Chevy or a Ford. Actually, God could very well have a reason for which one I should buy. If I were seriously dependent on Him and waited and watched for His answer, it could be one of those times where I would be blessed by seeing Him active in my life.

Answers could come through reading, studying, and counsel from others. Now, I may be greatly desirous of going forward with a project, but sometimes it may not be in God's timing. These thoughts tell us God wants to share our lives with Him. We know He created us, loves us, has plans for us, and wants us to be more dependent and resting in Him.

Abide

A major way to avoid the pitfalls and traps in life, is to "abide" in Jesus Christ so as to flourish and grow. Jesus uses the parable of the vine and the branches to show the necessity of abiding in Him (John 15: 1-9). In verse 9, He also says *"abide in My love."* The word "abiding" leads me to think of living and depending on God as well as His protecting and empowering us.

Just like fruits and vegetables need the plant to exist and grow, we must be attached to the life giver, God. Please don't overlook God's admonition spoken through the apostle Paul to all of us: *"Therefore, my beloved brethren, be steadfast, immovable, always abounding in the work of the Lord, knowing that your labor is not in vain in the Lord"* (1 Cor. 15:58).

Reconciliation

Another word that has become paramount in my thinking is reconciliation. The fact that we are set free from the bondage and guilt of sin, found through the blood of Jesus Christ, is an unmatched gift from God with no equal. The other element of this salvation is that we are then reconciled with God, whom we were once separated from by our sin, and now He lives within us through the power of the Holy Spirit.

The word means not just into a good relationship in general, but by our being forgiven of sin, including words and actions that bring hate and separation. I knew I was a Christian for many years, but seeing myself as reconciled to God gives me a greater understanding of who I am in relationship with God. I am loved by Him, adopted into His "family." He guides me, pours out His grace on me, comforts me, and assures me of His love for me. This brings us hope. Praise God!

Dependence

We know the concept of something being weaker and needing something stronger to lift or stabilize it. This is also a picture of us. We are greatly in need of Jesus Christ, not only in guiding and sustaining us, but also in guaranteeing eternal life to those who believe in Him as Lord and Savior. This dependence on Him will help us become stronger and infinitely wiser. We will also grow in our knowledge of Him. This comes through reading God's Word, Bible study, church participation, worship and fellowship with believers. God put us on the earth to love and be dependent on Him.

Sharing & Witnessing

Remember when you first fell in love? You couldn't stop telling everyone you knew about it. Or your favorite sports figure, any time they did anything outstanding you had to tell fans or followers of that sport. When you graduated, how did you feel? You had to tell someone. We all love to tell others things that are important to us.

Becoming a Christian was, to most, a great move into a new life. We shared that event with all who understood what that means. Now, as we go through our day-to-day routines and various things happen with us, can we recognize God in them, or are they just everyday happenings? When we land a new and exciting job or find a great deal on a new home or car, we are thrilled and share this with others. How about accomplishing a goal you really wanted to reach? Or maybe a schedule you had to meet that was tough to accomplish.

There are times we take as routine, but where was God in these times? Were you asking God to assist you? Why not? Maybe you had to modify some part of it, but you were still successful. God cares for us in all these situations we get into. He wants to be a part of our lives, but we need to allow Him. We can, and should, be rejoicing in His grace and mercy and sharing these experiences with others.

As we grow in our understanding of God and His grace and mercy, we will see that He wants and looks for us to depend on Him and rejoice as our loads in daily life are lightened or relieved. Then, we want others to know we have a caring and loving God.

The growth in our spiritual lives lead us to share and be witnesses to those who don't know the kind of God we believe and rest in. We shouldn't be worried with not being able to quote book-chapter and verse from God's Word. Most people will enjoy hearing what's going on in your life or what you have found beneficial.

1 Chronicles 16:8-12 says, *"Oh, give thanks to the Lord! Call upon His name; Make known His deeds among the peoples! Sing to Him, sing psalms to Him; Talk of all His wondrous works! Glory in His holy name; Let the hearts of those rejoice who seek the Lord! Seek the Lord and His strength; Seek His face evermore! Remember His marvelous works which He has done, His wonders, and the judgments of His mouth!"*

Joy

Possibly one of the most personally beneficial characteristics found in scriptures is joy. *"You will show me the path of life; In your presence is fullness of joy; At your right hand are pleasures forevermore"* (Ps. 16:11). This leads to not just an emotional statement but will bring joy and conviction in our journey to heavenly eternity. Joy should be found in the believer's daily life as well as in the church. *"These things I have spoken to you, that My joy may remain in you, and that your joy may full"* (John 15:11).

Joy is more a state of well-being while happiness is usually found in a temporal situation. I may be eighty years old and feeling the aches, pains, and limitations that come with the years, but there is joy in my heart when I think of the many promises God has given to us in His Word. In Galatians 5:22, the apostle Paul referred to joy as one of the fruits of the Spirit.

Hope

We all hope for things or situations as they come up. We wish for opportunities. Some even bet such and such will happen. When hope is in the biblical sense, it is used with a foundation of belief. The best is yet to come; Jesus is coming again. This hope is built on teaching from the Bible. The hope Abraham had in Sarah giving birth at her age was justified by his belief in God. As it is said in Romans 4:18: *"who, contrary to hope, in hope believed, so that he became the father of many nations, according to what was spoken, So shall your descendants be."*

Our Christian lives are being led by our hope in God's Word. He has created us and established us at this time and location.

Now He is guiding us through a fulfilled life toward an unmanageable eternity. This is hope!

Eternity

As I consider the concept of hope, I think about why we are here and how we are preparing for our eternity. We hope and believe in God for our daily and future needs. This is the way it should be. As we continue to grow in a deeper and more satisfying relationship with dependance on Him, we mustn't fail to realize that all of this experience and growth is preparing us for our eternity with Him. We can be enjoying a "taste of Heaven" as we are living day-to-day in this fallen world.

Knowing Jesus as our advocate, we can trust Him for His guidance, which gives us peace and confidence. Remember, this peace comes from reading and believing God's Word. His Word also leads us into thinking about our eternity and trusting in His promises for not only now, but forever. Through my understanding of God's Word, these wonderful times I now have with Him, are just a "taste of Heaven" with which God has in store for us for eternity.

Charles Stanley says things in a manner I wish I could: *"This life on earth is not as good as it gets, there is more for you in eternity."* In your present situation, joys may be mingled with sorrows, but one day pain and tears will be eliminated. The best is unquestionably yet to come.

Other Thoughts

Look at yourself in the way God does, before your conversion from a "sinner," and after your commitment to Him as a "believer." Now, see yourself as a child of God who has been redeemed by the blood of Jesus Christ. This shows God's all-inclusive love for you by bringing you into His family and giving you eternal life through His Son. We may sometimes take that for granted during our day-to-day activities. **CAUTION!**

As you consider God, look at Him in His fullness. He is your Creator, Lover of your soul, Savior, Provider, Director, Enlightener, Giver of wisdom, Companion, Comforter, Healer, Listener, and more! Do you really consider these attributes of God being available to guide you through life? Please, don't forget God's promise to be with us at "all" times. He doesn't intend for us to go through life on our own. I think many of us just don't realize this.

He wants an intimate relationship with you. Closer than you could ever consider. A while back, Charles Stanley shared a sermon in which I have encapsulated into three words for me to live by: **BELIEVE, TRUST, OBEY.** Many times, I have needed to repeat these three words to myself and others. How can we trust and obey God if we don't really believe the words He says? It just doesn't work that way.

Recap

- He needs you to believe in Him.
- He longs for you to trust Him.
- He longs for you to be obedient to Him.
- Listen to Him, throughout the day, in prayer and all situations you find yourself in.
- Depend on Him at all times. If you can't, why not? This can bring freedom and lifts the heavy burdens from your shoulders.
- *"Rejoice always, pray without ceasing, in everything give thanks; for this the will of God in Christ Jesus for you"* (1 Thes. 5:16-18).

- "Look" for God being present throughout your day and thank Him as you recognize and understand His presence.
- Include Him in all your thoughts and needs.
- *"Rejoice in the Lord always. Again, I will say, rejoice"* (Philippians 4:4).
- Share the Good News of Jesus our Lord with others.

When I was nearly finished with this book, I read the following devotion from Dr. Charles Stanley's devotional book titled, *Jesus Our Perfect Hope*. After reading it I saw he had really captured what I was saying and felt it would be a great way to end this book.

Demonstrate Reverence August 4

"At times, the decisions you'll have to make will be important but difficult. Thankfully, the Lord is willing to give you clear guidance about every choice in your life. So why don't more Christians take advantage of this astounding privilege?

Although the promise of God's direction is an incredible gift, it will not really make a difference to us unless we truly believe that God is perfect in knowledge, all-sufficient in strength, unfailing in character, and unconditionally loving toward us.

This is key to trusting Him for our futures because He requires us to respect Him as God. We must honor what He says because of who He is.

Reverence to the Lord means you hold Him in higher esteem than you do yourself. You *"trust in the Lord with all your heart and do not lean on your own understanding"* (Pro. 3:5). In other words, you acknowledge that He has greater authority and wisdom than you do, and you trust Him to the point of obedience.

Are you facing a difficult situation? Analyze your attitude toward the Lord. Do you really have reverence for Him? Then respect Him as God and do what He says."

"Jesus, I humble myself before You. I will obey You fully–show me what to do. Amen"

Closing

"Is that all there is?" speaks loudly to me when I reflect on that title. When I equate that thinking with my Christian life today, it leads me to consider the life God has been leading me through. He started by inviting me into His family! He has shown me He loves me. He has inspired me. He has provided me with the most comprehensive teaching tool in the world, the Bible. He has healed me, both physically and spiritually. He has encouraged me. He has guided me. He has forgiven me. And very importantly, given me hope. Even in this day of great uncertainty, look to Him!

Our questions or dissatisfaction should cause us to look at all He has done for us and is continually doing. Also, we realize that He is not finished with us. Paul wrote in Philippians, *"being confident of this very thing, that He who has begun a good work in you will complete it until the day of Jesus Christ"* (Phi. 1:6). God has brought us into this world and offered us a full, and what promises to be, a most significant life here and a perfect eternal life, if only we believe Him!

As you have gone through what I have shared with you, you may have read something that brings to you some personal concern. Please, take it first to our heavenly Father. He longs for a personal relationship with you that includes both His love and care, as well as your understanding of Him for now and through eternity. I sincerely pray that God will bless you as you reflect on this book.

I trust that you will pour out your heart to God and see Him as David did throughout Psalm 145.

In this psalm, David praised God for who He is, what He has done, and what He has promised.

DON'T FORGET

In this fallen world we live in, with all its trials and sufferings, God wants to lead you through into a productive, joyful, and peaceful life!

www.ingramcontent.com/pod-product-compliance
Ingram Content Group UK Ltd.
Pitfield, Milton Keynes, MK11 3LW, UK
UKHW041948230426
12048UKWH00008B/202